Learning in the Round: Moving Forward in the Restorative Classroom
—A Circle RP Resource

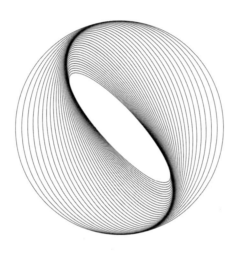

Authors
David Sullivan-Konyn, MA
Catherine Sullivan-Konyn, MSW

Editor
Teresa Heier, MILS

Illustrator and Designer
Nakeysha Roberts Washington, M.S. Ed
Genre Urban Arts, LLC

Co-Designer
Shaunteri Skinner

Copyright © 2021 by David Sullivan-Konyn, MA, Teresa Heier, MILS, and Nakeysha Roberts Washington, M.S. Ed

To obtain copies of Learning in the Round: Moving Forward in the Restorative Classroom- a Circle RP Resource, please contact the publisher:

CircleRP, LLC.
4218 North 13th Street
Milwaukee, WI 53209
www.TheCircleRP.com

All rights reserved. No part of this book may be reproduced or distributed, stored in a database or a retrieval system, or transmitted in any form or by any means, electronic, mechanical, photocopying, recording, or otherwise, without the prior written permission of CircleRP, LLC.

Manufactured and printed in the United States of America.
ISBN: 978-1-7370863-0-7

Table of Contents

Lesson	Activities	Page
	Foreword: *Learning in the Round* by David Sullivan-Konyn	4
1	Introducing Learning Circles in Schools 1.2	8
2	Introducing the Talking Piece 1.3	11
3	Circle for Making a Talking Piece 1.4	14
4	Practicing the Use of the Talking Piece 1.5	17
5	Building Our Circle Skills 1.6	20
6	Creating a Safe and Happy Classroom Circle 2.1	23
7	Circle for Designing Our Classroom Community to Meet Our Needs 2.2	26
8	Exploring Our Values-in-Action Circles 2.3	29
9	Coming to Consensus on Classroom Agreements Circle 2.4	32
10	Progress Check of Myself and of My Classroom 2.6	35
11	Understanding and Living with School Rules Circle 2.7	38
12	Relationships 101 Circle 4.8	41
13	Celebration Circle 4.2	44
14	Showing Gratitude and Appreciation Circle 4.3	47
15	What is Friendship? Circle 4.5	50
16	The Road to Success in the Learning Circle 4.7	53
17	Exploring Dimensions of Our Identity Circle 4.9	56
18	Elements of a Healthy Relationship Circle 4.11	59
19	"You Win Some, You Lose Some" Reflection Circle 4.14-4.15	62
20	"Listen to the Silence, It Has Much to Say" Silence Circle 5.1	65
21	Who Am I Really? Circle 5.7	68
22	What Motivates You? Circle 6.1	71
23	Relationships 102 Circle 10.1	74
24	What Went Right in Your Family Circle 10.6	77
25	Identifying Sources of Support Circle 10.7	80

Foreword

Learning in the Round: Moving Forward in the Restorative Classroom is the first of its kind guide for our students who learn in circle in the restorative classroom. It includes more than seventy-five activities and reflections designed to enhance the restorative journey of personal growth and empowerment that our students take for an entire school year. Designed as a resource to be utilized in any restorative classroom, *Learning in the Round* rests upon the inspirational shoulders of the most comprehensive restorative teaching resource currently available: *Circle Forward: Building a Restorative School Community*, by Carolyn Boyes-Watson and Kay Pranis. They guide educators through the practice of restorative teaching with their straightforward lessons for almost any classroom situation with grace and dignity. The resources in *Learning in the Round* compliment and demonstrate how our students' personal growth can be successfully nurtured, developed, and documented in the restorative way.

Our school, Barack Obama School of Career and Technical Education, embarked upon a mission to become a restorative practice school in 2016. Then our school district sent my colleagues and I to the National Association of Community and Restorative Justice Conference in Oakland, California. Among the few thousand aspiring Restorative Practices' practitioners at the conference, I experienced an epiphany in my teaching practices. A teaching resource caught my eye entitled, *Circle Forward*. It appeared to have dozens of ready-made restorative lesson plans. Being the type of teacher that is always on the lookout for new, ready-made lesson plans, I pulled out my wallet and handed the super-nice lady, Loretta, my credit card. In one of the breakout sessions, the presenters were asked if they knew of any teachers who taught exclusively in circles. Their answer was something along the lines of "Sure, there is this person doing circles all the time at so-and-so school, but they were not teaching exclusively in circles..., yet it would surely be awesome if someone did!" I decided at that moment that I would strive to teach all of my lessons in all of my classes, everyday, in circle. *Circle Forward* would provide the blueprint I needed to make this lofty goal a successful reality.

Upon our return to Milwaukee, I made steady but slow progress with my students, often taking one-step forward followed by stumbling two-steps back. I realized that I faced some significant challenges that held us back from taking learning in circle to the next level. At first, many students refrained from sharing in front of others, even at the most conversational level. Some would not even join the learning circle and moved their chairs to the other side of the room where they refused to participate. Secondly, I found that some students who would not share aloud under any circumstances would at least write their thoughts, ideas, and feelings down on paper much more readily. Yet, even if things were really going well, I would have scant evidence of the immense progress my students were making in creating a tolerant and vibrant learning community. I often found myself enthusiastically explaining to my colleagues all the wonderful thoughts and ideas my students were sharing in our learning circles. But without some tangible evidence of student work, few of my colleagues embarked upon the potential benefits of teaching in circle in their own classrooms.

My solution was the time-tested go-to teacher strategy: the class worksheet. I decided to create my own version of sneaky worksheets. My "sneaky sheets" would pose thought-provoking questions and engaging activities to address the subjects of the next learning circle topic. It gave my students the opportunity to take a moment to think about what they might like to share before the next learning circle. My intentions were to have my students prepare what they wanted to say, and in turn, enhance the quality of the learning dialogues that we would have in the following learning circle. Next, they would get to work on an activity that would build their skills based on what we discussed in the learning circle. Finally, I developed reflection questions that I hoped would reinforce our progress, provide feedback on our learning circle process, and demonstrate the personal growth my students were making in class while also providing solid evidence of my students' progress over time.

This five-year-long project became *Learning in the Round*. This restorative practices guide will compliment students' work in your restorative classroom. Please join our Learning Community at TheCircleRP.com; your suggestions on how we can make *Learning in the Round* better are most appreciated. I would like to thank Catherine Sullivan-Konyn, Teresa Heier, and Nakeysha Roberts Washington, without whose help *Learning in the Round* could not have become a reality. A special thanks to Loretta Draths and Denise Breton from Living Justice Press whose support and counsel has been invaluable for this and many other past adventures. And a special thanks to Carolyn Boyes-Watson and Kay Pranis, co-authors of *Circle Forward*, for their pioneering restorative work. Finally, we must also thank all of our students who always and in all ways inspire us, teach us, and make us better people. As Whitney sang with her angelic voice, "Children are the future, let them lead the way!"

HOW TO USE THIS GUIDE:

All of the activities in *Learning in the Round* are broken into three categories for your stand alone restorative lesson(s) or in conjunction with the corresponding lesson in *Circle Forward* by title and module number. Each beginning activity is made up of 3-5 Pre-Circle reflective questions that students can answer before the circle lesson in class or as an entry ticket or *Do Now!* activity. Next, a circle activity or exercise follows that builds upon the theme of the day's learning circle lesson. The circle activity may be worked on as a whole-class or small group activity. Finally, there are another 4-5 Post-Circle reflection questions that students can answer as an exit ticket or completed as homework based on the learning circle topic. Using this guide will amaze both students and teachers with the documented progress made in the course of one years' restorative journey! ~David Sullivan-Konyn

WHO ARE YOU DEDICATING YOUR WORK OF ART TO?

Name: Date:

Section:

A dedication for a book gives a shout out to everyone who helped and supported the author in their labor of love. You can dedicate this work to one person or many people. You decide.

Who has had your back no matter what?

How have they helped you become the person who you are today?

You can also share what these people have meant to you and how they have helped you through their love.

What lessons have they afforded you that have made the difference in your success and in your life?

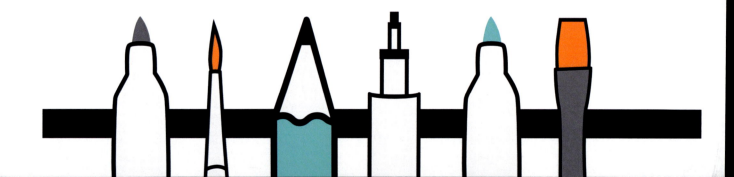

I, _____,
dedicate my work of art herein to
_____.

INTRODUCING LEARNING CIRCLES IN SCHOOLS 1.2

PRE-CIRCLE: *The following questions will help prepare you for the next learning circle.*

1. Have you ever participated in a Restorative Practice learning circle before? What was that experience like?

2. If you have not participated in a Restorative Practice learning circle before, then what do you know about Restorative Practice principles?

3. When we participate in a learning circle, we will listen and talk by listening from the heart and speaking from the heart. What does listening from the heart mean to you?

4. How is speaking and listening from the heart different and/or similar to other times when we communicate with each other?

INTRODUCING LEARNING CIRCLES IN SCHOOLS

CIRCLE ACTIVITY: *This activity will help you practice the concepts from today's learning circle.*

Directions: List 4 reasons or times when speaking and listening from your heart is important.

SPEAKING FROM YOUR HEART...

1.

2.

3.

4.

LISTENING FROM YOUR HEART...

1.

2

3.

4.

INTRODUCING LEARNING CIRCLES IN SCHOOLS

POST-CIRCLE: *Reflect on today's learning circle.*

1. What went well in today's learning circle? Describe the style of communicating in the learning circle.

2. How can we improve future learning circles?

3. How do you feel about what you shared in the learning circle today?

4. Is there anything you wish you could have shared but did not share in the learning circle today?

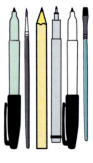

INTRODUCING THE TALKING PIECE 1.3

PRE-CIRCLE: *The following questions will help you prepare for the next learning circle.*

1. Using a Talking Piece allows each person to be heard when they speak. Think of a time when you had something to say and felt heard. Describe what that was like.

2. Now think about a time when you had something important to say and did not feel heard. Describe what this was like.

3. Listening from the heart takes discipline and practice. If you expect others to listen with respect to you, then why is it important that we listen with respect to others?

4. What is something that you feel is important to you that you could share in the learning circle if others listened with respect to you?

INTRODUCING THE TALKING PIECE

CIRCLE ACTIVITY: This activity helps you practice the concepts from the learning circle.

Using the Talking Piece in Learning Circle

When someone has the Talking Piece, I HEAR...	...and that makes me THINK...

Describe your thoughts about using the talking piece in class.

INTRODUCING THE TALKING PIECE

POST-CIRCLE: *Reflect on today's learning circle.*

1. What did you notice about using the talking piece in today's learning circle?

2. How do people speak when they are using the talking piece?

3. How does it make you feel when you must listen while someone else has the talking piece and you cannot just speak what is on your mind?

4. Did what you shared in the learning circle change when you had to wait for the talking piece to speak?

CIRCLE FOR MAKING A TALKING PIECE 1.4

PRE-CIRCLE: *The following questions will help you prepare for the next learning circle.*

1. Why is it important to use a talking piece in the learning circle?

2. Why do you think communicating is different when using a talking piece in the learning circle?

3. What does using a talking piece in the learning circle mean for you when you have something important to share?

4. Think about a difficult conversation you have had before. Did you have the opportunity to speak without interruption? How would have using a talking piece been helpful during this conversation?

5. What will your talking piece say about you as a person?

CIRCLE FOR MAKING A TALKING PIECE

CIRCLE ACTIVITY: *This activity will help you practice the concepts from today's learning circle.*

Directions: Draw what your personal talking piece would look like below.

CIRCLE FOR MAKING A TALKING PIECE

POST-CIRCLE: *Reflect on today's learning circle.*

1. Describe the talking piece you created today. Explain why your talking piece is important to you.

2. In learning circle, what were you able to share about the talking piece that you created today?

3. If you did not share in learning circle today, what would you have said if you would have had the chance?

4. How did your peers do in learning circle today? What do you think the circle needs?

PRACTICING THE USE OF THE TALKING PIECE CIRCLE 1.5

PRE-CIRCLE: *The following questions will help you prepare for the next learning circle.*

1. What does it feel like to have your peers really listen with respect to you in the learning circle?

2. How does it feel to really listen with respect to what your peers say in the learning circle?

3. Why is it important to take turns speaking in the learning circle?

4. How is the process of communicating in the learning circle different from how we normally speak with each other?

PRACTICING THE USE OF THE TALKING PIECE CIRCLE

CIRCLE ACTIVITY: *This activity will help you practice the concepts from today's learning circle.*

Directions: In the boxes below, take time to reflect on your life and respond to the questions.

A. What is your purpose in life today?

B. What do you have faith in today?

C. What do you place your hope in for tomorrow?

PRACTICING THE USE OF THE TALKING PIECE CIRCLE

POST-CIRCLE: *Reflect on today's learning circle.*

1. What have you noticed about how you and your peers act when using the talking piece in learning circles thus far?

2. How does it feel to really listen with respect to your peers when they share in the learning circle?

3. Why do you think it is important to be able to speak without being interrupted when you have the talking piece in the learning circle?

4. What questions should be asked by members of your class community about the learning circle that have not been asked yet?

BUILDING OUR CIRCLE SKILLS 1.6

PRE-CIRCLE: *The following questions will help you prepare for the next learning circle.*

1. What are some communication skills that you would like to improve at in the learning circle? Some examples might include: listening from the heart, speaking from the heart, challenging your beliefs, or accepting others' perspectives. Explain why.

2. How do you know when someone is listening with their heart when you are speaking?

3. How do you know if someone is speaking from their heart in learning circle?

4. Discuss a time when someone listened with their heart about something you shared. What did that feel like?

BUILDING OUR CIRCLE SKILLS

CIRCLE ACTIVITY: *This activity will help you practice the concepts from in today's learning circle.*

Directions: After participating in the circle, reflect on your skills. In each box, write 1 skill that you do well and one that challenges you.

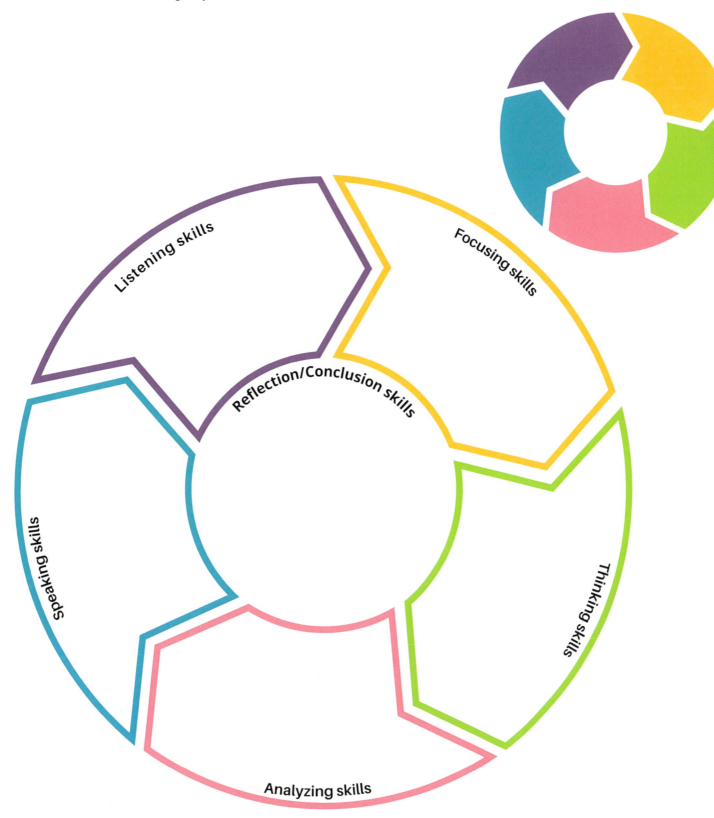

BUILDING OUR CIRCLE SKILLS

POST-CIRCLE: *Reflect on today's learning circle.*

1. What felt right in the learning circle today? What can be done to make sure that good things happen all the time in the learning circle?

2. Think about what it was like to listen and speak from your heart. How did that make you feel?

3. How can you practice listening and speaking from your heart in other conversions and situations?

4. What are one or two conversations or situations in your life that would be improved if you practiced listening and speaking from your heart?

CREATING A SAFE AND HAPPY CLASSROOM CIRCLE 2.1

PRE-CIRCLE: *The following questions will help you prepare for the next learning circle.*

1. What does it mean to feel safe and happy to you?

2. Why is it important to you and your peers to feel safe and happy in class and in the learning circle?

3. When do you feel safe and happy in class? In what class do you currently feel the most at ease in? Why?

4. In the class that you feel most at ease in, what qualities of this class make it feel safe and happy?

CREATING A SAFE AND HAPPY CLASSROOM CIRCLE

CIRCLE ACTIVITY: *This activity will help you practice the concepts from today's learning circle.*

Directions: In the spaces provided, describe what a happy classroom looks like, sounds like, feels like, and what it is not.

Looks like...

Sounds like...

My Safe and Happy Classroom

Feels like...

Is not...

CREATING A SAFE AND HAPPY CLASSROOM CIRCLE

POST-CIRCLE: *Reflect on today's learning circle.*

1. What is one thing you discovered in today's learning circle that you did not expect?

2. What was something one of your peers shared about feeling safe and happy in the classroom that you have not thought about before?

3. How can you help your peers feel safe and confident in class? Does that mean you will need to change or do more of what you already do?

4. How can your peers make you feel safe, happy, and comfortable in class? Is that happening now? If not, what can they do to make that happen?

CIRCLE FOR DESIGNING OUR CLASSROOM COMMUNITY TO MEET OUR NEEDS 2.2

PRE-CIRCLE: *The following questions will help you prepare for the next learning circle.*

1. What do you need to be academically, socially, and mentally successful in class?

2. How do you need to be treated by your peers in the learning circle?

3. How do you need to be treated by your teacher in the learning circle?

4. What would a successful classroom community look like and be like?

CIRCLE FOR DESIGNING OUR CLASSROOM COMMUNITY TO MEET OUR NEEDS

CIRCLE ACTIVITY: *This activity will help you practice the concepts from today's learning circle.*

Directions: In the chart below, draw the items that you would need to support your best learning environment.

Directions: Now, list the items included in your drawing and explain the importance of them.

CIRCLE FOR DESIGNING OUR CLASSROOM COMMUNITY TO MEET OUR NEEDS

POST-CIRCLE: *Reflect on today's learning circle.*

1. What is one positive thing you learned about one of your peers in today's learning circle that you did not know before?

2. What is one way that you can help your peers to be more academically successful in your class community?

3. What is one way that your peers can help you be more academically successful in your class community?

4. What is one way that you can help your teacher make your class community more academically successful?

EXPLORING OUR VALUES-IN-ACTION CIRCLES 2.3

PRE-CIRCLE: *The following questions will help you prepare for the next learning circle.*

1. List the top five values that you live your life by:

2. Where do your values come from: your parents, your family, your friends, your mentors, or inside youself?

3. Why are shared values or norms an important part of a classroom community and in learning circles?

4. What values or norms do you think would make this a successful educational community this year? Why?

EXPLORING OUR VALUES-IN-ACTION CIRCLES

CIRCLE ACTIVITY: *This activity will you practice the concepts from today's learning circle.*

Directions: Using the list below or other values, rank your three most important values on the lines below.

WHAT VALUES ARE IMPORTANT TO YOU?

Getting good grades
Making a lot of friends
Having one best friend
Having a good relationship with
my parents
Making a good living
Having good relationships with
all of my family members
Having enough time to myself
Having enough to eat
Getting a good job

Liking my job
Respecting myself
Respecting others
Being respected by others
Having good health
Falling in love
Having stylish clothes
Getting into shape
Helping other people
Your own: _____
Your own: _____

Rank the three most important values in your life:

_____

_____

_____

Why did you pick those three values?

_____

_____

_____

EXPLORING OUR VALUES-IN-ACTION CIRCLES

POST-CIRCLE: *Reflect on today's learning circle.*

1. What is one thing you learned about one of your peers' values in the learning circle that you did not know before?

2. What values do you agree with that were shared in the learning circle? Why?

3. What values do you disagree with that were shared in the learning circle? Why?

4. How can you help others be accountable for their values that they shared in the learning circle?

COMING TO CONSENSUS ON CLASSROOM AGREEMENTS CIRCLE 2.4

PRE-CIRCLE: *The following questions will help you prepare for the next learning circle.*

1. What does it mean to you to do your best at something?

2. How do you know that you are doing your best instead of just doing enough?

3. What norms do you agree with to make your classroom community a great place to learn?

4. What is one norm that you would find challenging to follow? Explain why.

COMING TO CONSENSUS ON CLASSROOM AGREEMENTS CIRCLE

CIRCLE ACTIVITY: *This activity helps you practice the concepts from today's learning circle.*

Ranking Your Classroom Agreements

Write out your Classroom Agreements List in the boxes below. Then rank your classroom agreements between 1-5.   5 = easy to follow.   1=too difficult to follow.

Give three examples in your life where considering the interests of others is a priority.

-
-
-

COMING TO CONSENSUS ON CLASSROOM AGREEMENTS CIRCLE

POST-CIRCLE: *Reflect on today's learning circle.*

1. Which of these classroom agreements would be easiest for you to honor?

2. Which of these classroom agreements would be hard for you to honor?

3. What support would help you to honor the classroom agreements you mentioned above as being hard to honor?

4. Are there any classroom agreement norms that you refuse to honor at this time? Why?

PROGRESS CHECK OF MYSELF AND OF MY CLASSROOM 2.6

PRE-CIRCLE: *The following questions will help you prepare for the next learning circle.*

1. How do you feel about your participation in the learning circles up to this point? What are your thoughts on this way of learning?

2. How does sharing in the Learning Circle empower your voice within our classroom community?

3. Have you noticed your confidence growing from sharing your views in learning circles?

4. How do you think the class is doing as a learning group?

5. What is going well in learning circles for our learning community? How can you help to make it better for everyone?

PROGRESS CHECK OF MYSELF AND MY CLASSROOM

Circle Activity: This activity will help you practice the concepts from today's learning circle.
Directions: Fill in the boxes below with pictures to illustrate your ideas.

Draw a cartoon of how you are feeling right now.

Draw a cartoon of how you take care of yourself or others in school.

Draw a cartoon of how you take care of your school.

PROGRESS CHECK OF MYSELF AND MY CLASSROOM

POST-CIRCLE: *Reflect on today's learning circle.*

1. What are some values, norms, and class agreements that your classroom community does well with?

2. What are some values, norms, and class agreements that your classroom community struggles with?

3. How can you support your classmates with the values, norms, and class agreements they are struggling with?

4. What could your teacher do to support the classroom community with the agreed upon values, norms, and class agreements?

UNDERSTANDING AND LIVING WITH SCHOOL RULES CIRCLE 2.7

PRE-CIRCLE: *The following questions will help you prepare for the next learning circle.*

1. Reflect and write out one of your school's rules. What is the rule and why do you think it exists?

2. What is challenging about accepting and abiding by this rule?

3. What is a school rule that you or your peers find difficult to accept and abide by?

4. Why is this rule so difficult to to accept and abide by? How could you rework this rule to make it acceptable?

UNDERSTANDING AND LIVING WITH
SCHOOL RULES CIRCLE

CIRCLE ACTIVITY: *This activity will help you practice the concepts from today's learning circle.*

Directions: In the chart below, list one of the school rules discussed in circle. Write the pros and cons of that rule.

School Rule:

Pros	Cons

What is a school rule that you or your peers find difficult to follow? Why do you think this is so?

UNDERSTANDING AND LIVING WITH SCHOOL RULES CIRCLE

POST-CIRCLE: *Reflect on today's learning circle.*

1. How can you support your peers to accept and abide by your school's rules?

2. How does accepting and abiding by your school's rules support your learning community?

3. What is a school rule that everyone agrees needs to be changed? How can you change this school rule in a constructive way?

4. What other school rules need to be re-examined or changed? Why?

RELATIONSHIPS 101 CIRCLE 4.8

PRE-CIRCLE: *The following questions will help you prepare for the next learning circle.*

1. What has been going well for you this past week, or what is something that you are looking forward to?

2. Who is a person you can rely on and trust? What are their personality characteristics?

3. What traits make a strong friendship? Why?

4. Why do some relationships not work out?

RELATIONSHIPS 101 CIRCLE

CIRCLE ACTIVITY: *This activity helps you practice the concepts from today's learning circle.*

Directions: The pieces connect together to make up all of the characteristics of building a strong relationship. Fill in the puzzle pieces with character traits you feel are important to a strong relationship.

RELATIONSHIPS 101 CIRCLE

POST-CIRCLE: *Reflect on today's learning circle.*

1. Why is it important to build relationships in the classroom and school?

2. What are the qualities you bring to your friendships?

3. What can you do to make yourself a better friend?

4. Make a list of your friends to thank them for all they have done for you.

CELEBRATION CIRCLE 4.2

PRE-CIRCLE: *The following questions will help you prepare for the next learning circle.*

1. What will you be celebrating in the learning circle today?

2. What type of celebration will you have and who will participate in your celebration?

3. List three ways in which celebrating our peers in the learning circle builds community.

4. What is an upcoming achievement you will accomplish in the near future and how will you celebrate it?

CELEBRATION CIRCLE

CIRCLE ACTIVITY: This activity will help you practice the concepts from today's learning circle.

Directions: Describe the layers of your celebration. Start with the celebration at the top then describe the important steps leading up to the event.

CELEBRATION CIRCLE

POST-**CIRCLE:** *Reflect on today's learning circle.*

1. What was the cause for celebration in today's learning circle?

2. Briefly explain what happened in the celebration learning circle today.

3. How does participating in a celebration learning circle change the climate of your classroom community and in your school?

4. Describe a celebration that honored you in some way. What did it fell like to be recognized by others for your accomplishment(s)?

SHOWING GRATITUDE AND APPRECIATION CIRCLE 4.3

PRE-CIRCLE: *The following questions will help you prepare for the next learning circle.*

1. What does it mean to you to show gratitude for others?

2. Who are you grateful for today? Why?

3. What is something you appreciate about yourself?

4. How do you show appreciation for those in your community that work with you?

SHOWING GRATITUDE AND APPRECIATION CIRCLE

CIRCLE ACTIVITY: *This activity will help you practice the concepts from today's learning circle.*

Directions: Write a thank you letter to someone who you would like to express your appreciation to. Be sure to give them a copy of your letter.

Dear _____ , _____

_____

_____

_____

_____

_____

_____

_____

_____

_____

_____

_____

_____

_____

_____

_____

_____

_____

_____

_____

_____

_____

_____

Thank you again, _____

_____

SHOWING GRATITUDE AND APPRECIATION CIRCLE

POST-CIRCLE: *Reflect on today's learning circle.*

1. What was shared by your classmates in learning circle about what it means to show gratitude and appreciation?

2. Briefly explain what happened in the Showing Gratitude and Appreciation learning circle today.

3. What were your peers grateful for? What was a common thread with many of the students?

4. Describe someone who deserves to be honored, but has not experienced the appreciation of others for their accomplishments. What can you do so they could be appropriately recognized?

WHAT IS FRIENDSHIP? CIRCLE 4.5

PRE-CIRCLE: *The following questions will help you prepare for the next learning circle.*

1. What qualities or values do you look for in a friend? Circle as many as needed:

   Compassion   Creativity   Honesty   Integrity   Love   Loyalty

   Privacy   Confidence   Kindness   Self-Respect   Trust   Wisdom

2. What is the most important quality of a best friend? Why?

3. What does "being a great friend" mean to you?

4. How are you a great friend to others?

WHAT IS FRIENDSHIP?

CIRCLE ACTIVITY: *This activity will help you practice the concepts from today's learning circle.*

Directions: Trace your hand below. Then write one character trait of a good friend in each finger.

WHAT IS FRIENDSHIP?

POST-CIRCLE: *Reflect on today's learning circle.*

1. What did you learn from hearing your peers share about what they value in friendships?

2. What is something you have not thought about before as it relates to "real friends" after participating in today's learning circle?

3. Have your views on what makes a "real friend" changed after listening in learning circle today? Why or why not?

4. Based on how the discussion went today in learning circle, will you be more confident in making new friends or more cautious? Why?

THE ROAD TO SUCCESS IN THE LEARNING CIRCLE 4.7

PRE-CIRCLE: *The following questions will help you prepare for the next learning circle.*

1. Think about someone who is successful in your life. What personality traits help them in their success?

2. What activities, pursuits, or hobbies make you feel content and happy when you do them? Why?

3. What provides you with greater satisfaction, engaging in an activity or enjoying the end result of it? Why?

4. What do you value more: something you worked really hard on and failed, or something you didn't put a lot of effort into and succeeded? Why?

THE ROAD TO SUCCESS IN THE LEARNING CIRCLE

CIRCLE ACTIVITY: *This activity will help you practice the concepts from today's learning circle.*

Directions: Create a list of characteristics that you feel contribute to personal success and record them in the squares below. Consider the characteristics of someone you look up to.

THE ROAD TO SUCCESS IN THE LEARNING CIRCLE

POST-CIRCLE: *Reflect on today's learning circle.*

1. What did most of your peers share in common as the definition of success in today's learning circle?

2. Do you agree with your classmates' definitions or do you have a different definition of success? Explain your answer in detail.

3. What are some **differences** between the meaning of success and the meaning of happiness?

4. What are some **similarities between** the meaning of success and the meaning of happiness?

EXPLORING DIMENSIONS OF OUR IDENTITY CIRCLE 4.9

PRE-CIRCLE: *The following questions will help you prepare for the next learning circle.*

1. If asked what makes you who you are, how would you answer?

2. If your classmates were asked to describe you, what would they say?

3. If your friends were asked to describe you, what would they say?

4. If your family was asked to describe you, what would they say?

EXPLORING DIMENSIONS OF OUR IDENTITY CIRCLE

CIRCLE ACTIVITY: *This activity will help you practice the concepts from today's earning circle.*

Directions:
In the inner circle, write down words that would describe yourself.
In the second circle, write down words that your family would use to describe who you are.
In the third circle, write down words that your friends would use to describe who you are.
Outside the circle, write down words that your community would use to describe who you are.

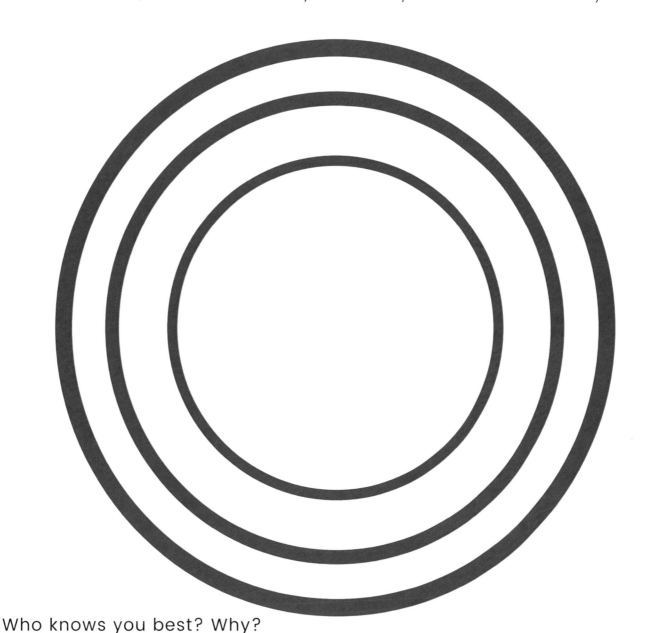

Who knows you best? Why?
_____
_____
_____
_____

EXPLORING DIMENSIONS OF OUR IDENTITY CIRCLE

POST-CIRCLE: *Reflect on today's learning circle.*

1. How did it feel to participate in today's learning circle? Did you learn something new about anyone else in class?

2. How does it feel when you share from heart about your true self?

3. Who knows you best not including yourself? Why?

4. With whom can you share your deepest thoughts and feelings? Describe the level of trust you have with that person.

ELEMENTS OF A HEALTHY RELATIONSHIP CIRCLE 4.11

PRE-CIRCLE: *The following questions will help you prepare for the next learning circle.*

1. Think about the relationships you have in your life. What are the healthy traits in those relationships?

2. Again, think about the relationships you have in your life. What are the traits that might be unhealthy?

3. Make a list of healthy versus unhealthy relationship traits.

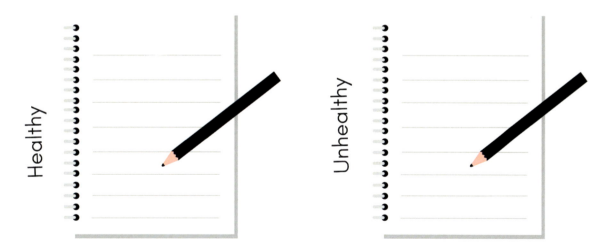

4. Who are the people in your life who are in healthy relationships? What do their relationship(s) look like from your perspective?

ELEMENTS OF A HEALTHY RELATIONSHIP CIRCLE

CIRCLE ACTIVITY: This activity will help you practice the concepts from today's learning circle.

Directions: Think of relationships/friendships in your life. What would you consider to be healthy and unhealthy? Write down the most important traits of a healthy relationship in the boxes below.

PEOPLE IN HEALTHY RELATIONSHIPS	TRAITS OF THOSE RELATIONSHIPS

Chose two people in your life who are in a healthy relationship.
Describe what that relationship looks like.

Based on what you discussed in learning circle, what is something you could do if you find yourself in an unhealthy relationship?

ELEMENTS OF A HEALTHY RELATIONSHIP CIRCLE

POST-CIRCLE: *Reflect on today's learning circle.*

1. Who can support you if you find yourself in an unhealthy relationship?

2. Briefly explain one take-away from the learning circle today.

3. Based on what you heard in today's learning circle, why is it important to maintain healthy relationships?

4. Chose a healthy relationship that your have in your life (family, friend, other). Describe the relationship and the person.

"YOU WIN SOME, YOU LOSE SOME" -AN ENGLISH PROVERB
REFLECTION CIRCLE 4.14-4.15

PRE-CIRCLE: *The following questions will help you prepare for the next learning circle.*

1. How does it feel to win a game with your team? How does it feel different than if you won a game in an individual sport?

2. How does it feel to lose a game with your team? How does it feel different than if you lose a game in an individual sport?

3. Share a time when you won or lost. Describe how you felt.

4. Based on your experience, do you feel that it's more important to win or to participate on a team even if you lost? Why?

"YOU WIN SOME, YOU LOSE SOME" -AN ENGLISH PROVERB
REFLECTION CIRCLE

CIRCLE ACTIVITY: This activity will help you practice the concepts from today's learning circle.

Directions: Reflect on winning and losing and complete the task below.

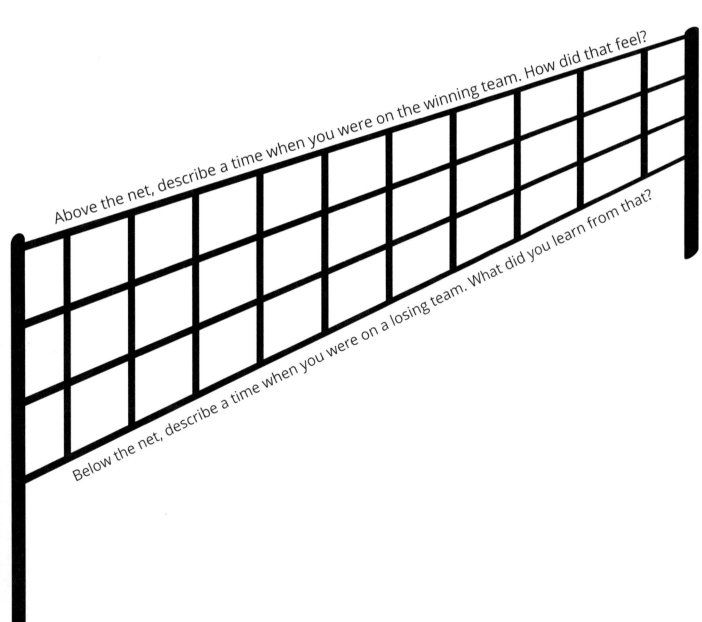

"YOU WIN SOME, YOU LOSE SOME" -AN ENGLISH PROVERB
REFLECTION CIRCLE

POST-CIRCLE: *The following questions will help you reflect on today's learning circle.*

1. Did your peers in learning circle think it was more important to be on a team to win or would they rather participate individually?

2. Did your thoughts on winning and losing change or stay the same after you participated in today's learning circle? Why or why not?

3. Based on what was shared in your learning circle today, do you feel that it's more important to win or to participate even if you lose? Why?

4. What team sports or individual sports have you participated in? What was your favorite memory from those times?

LISTEN TO THE SILENCE, IT HAS SO MUCH TO SAY. -RUMI
SILENCE CIRCLE 5.1

PRE-CIRCLE: *The following questions will help you prepare for the next learning circle.*

1. Where is the best place to quiet yourself to focus and reflect?

2. What is it about this place that helps you to calm yourself and to think deeply?

3. Are you able to go to this place regularly? Why or why not?

4. If you cannot go to your place of silence, is there another place where you can go to calm yourself and focus? Describe your alternate place for silence.

LISTEN TO THE SILENCE, IT HAS SO MUCH TO SAY. -RUMI
Silence Circle

CIRCLE ACTIVITY: *This activity will help you practice the concepts from today's learning circle.*

Directions: Draw what your place of peace and serenity looks like or draw what silence feels like. Consider where you can focus on silence, your breathing, and meditation. Your place of serenity can be inside or outside, cool or warm, but it should be calming and comfortable.

LISTEN TO THE SILENCE, IT HAS SO MUCH TO SAY. -RUMI
Silence Circle

POST-CIRCLE: *Reflect on today's learning circle.*

1. How does it feel when you are able to calmly think about things that are important to you? Do you feel that way after learning circle? Why or why not?

2. Are there things you think about that could become clearer if you were able to meditate more regularly?

3. How often are you able to meditate and sit in silence? If you have not had the opportunity to sit in silence and meditate, then will you be able to set aside a specific time everyday or every other day to meditate for 15-20 minutes each day?

4. Where and what time of the day would you be able to set aside the time to benefit from regular meditation sessions?

WHO AM I REALLY? CIRCLE 5.7

PRE-CIRCLE: *The following questions will help you prepare for the next learning circle.*

1. If someone asked you to describe yourself, what would you say?

2. Who really knows who you are? (Besides yourself of course!) What would they say about who you are?

3. What dreams do you have that would make your life more complete when they come true?

4. Describe how you can make your dreams come true.

WHO AM I REALLY?

CIRCLE ACTIVITY: *This activity will help you practice the concepts from today's learning circle.*

Directions: Fill in your shield with 5 words, symbols, or drawings that define who you are and decorate your shield.

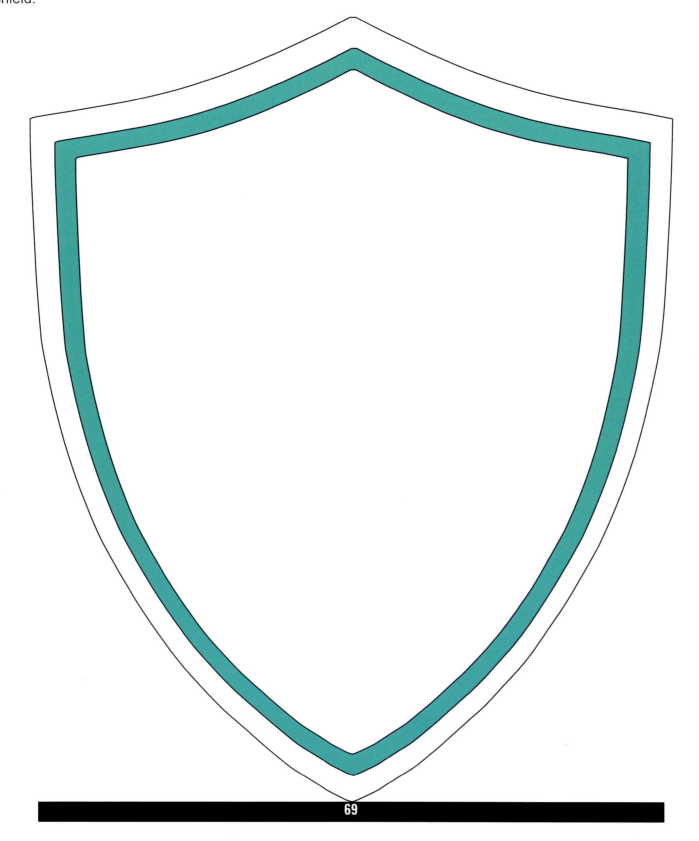

WHO AM I REALLY?

POST-CIRCLE: *Reflect on today's learning circle.*

1. What do you have in common with what your classmates shared about who they are?

2. Do you have similar dreams and goals as your peers? Explain.

3. Do you have different dreams and goals than your peers? Explain.

4. Some say that your true character is how you act when no one is watching. How do you act when no one is watching you?

WHAT MOTIVATES YOU? CIRCLE 6.1

PRE-CIRCLE: *The following questions will help you prepare for the next learning circle.*

1. What motivates you?

2. Give an example of a time you were motivated by your heart to do something.

3. Give an example of a time you were motivated by your head to do something.

4. Do you prefer to be motivated by your head or your heart? Why?

WHAT MOTIVATES YOU?

CIRCLE ACTIVITY: *This activity will help you practice the concepts from today's learning circle.*

Directions: In the speech bubble below, fill in what motivates you from your head and what motivates you from your heart.

What Motivates You...
   From your head?
   From your heart?

WHAT MOTIVATES YOU?

POST-CIRCLE: *Reflect on today's learning circle.*

1. How did today's learning circle help in identifying what motivates you and your peers?

2. Which motivates you more: developing relationships or accumulating personal possessions? Why?

3. Rank in the order of what motivates you most using numbers 1 through 4.

_____ personal goals and dreams

_____ accumulation of material possessions

_____ deepening relationships

_____ experiencing new situations

4. Do you think your motivations will change in the future? Explain.

RELATIONSHIPS 102 CIRCLE 10.1

PRE-CIRCLE: *The following questions will help you prepare for the next learning circle.*

1. Reflect and write about a time when you struggled to fit in.

2. What are some strengths that you bring to the learning circle?

3. How are relationships different from other relationships – friends,school, and work?

4. Would you like to learn more about your relationship tree?

RELATIONSHIPS 102 CIRCLE

CIRCLE ACTIVITY: This activity will helps you practice the concepts from in today's learning circle.

Directions: Fill in the names of the people in your relationship tree. You can include grandparents, parents, aunts, uncles, cousins, friends, and mentors! Feel free to add more boxes throughout the relationship tree.

Your Relationship Tree:

RELATIONSHIPS 102 CIRCLE

Post Circle: Reflect on today's learning circle.

1. Who are you closest to in your life? Why are you so close to them?

2. After working on your **relationship** tree, what do you notice about the people closest to you in your life?

3. What advice, support, and motivation can you get from your grandparents, parents, siblings, aunts, uncles, friends, and mentors?

4. What did you learn in today's circle about your peers' relationship trees?

WHAT WENT RIGHT IN YOUR FAMILY? CIRCLE 10.6

PRE-CIRCLE: *The following questions will help you prepare for the next learning circle.*

1. What is the best memory you have of your family together?

2. What does your family do together to have fun?

3. Where is your family's favorite place to go out to eat together, or what is the favorite meal that your family likes to have together?

4. Where have you and your family traveled to visit friends and relatives?

WHAT WENT RIGHT IN YOUR FAMILY?

CIRCLE ACTIVITY: *This activity helps you practice the concepts from today's learning circle.*

Directions: Pick 3 of your favorite people and name them. Write your favorite memory with each person below.

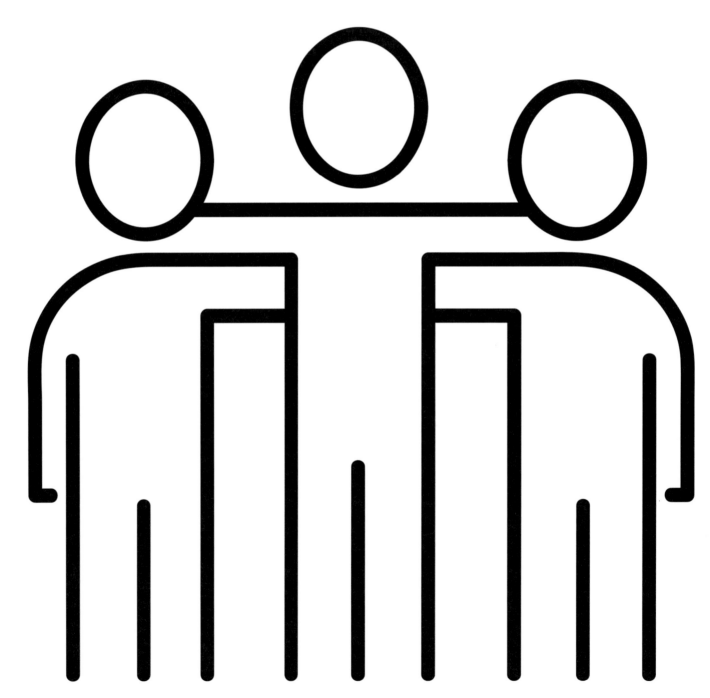

WHAT WENT RIGHT IN YOUR FAMILY?

POST-CIRCLE: *Reflect on today's learning circle.*

1. When you listen to your peers share about what went right with their families, how does it make you feel about your own family?

2. What went right with your family?

3. If things need to be mended with your family, what can you do to help make things right?

4. What do you want to do right when you have your own family?

IDENTIFYING SOURCES OF SUPPORT CIRCLE 10.7

PRE-CIRCLE: *The following questions will help you prepare for the next learning circle.*

1. Who do you ask for advice when you need supportive and productive guidance? Why do you count on the advice and guidance from them?

2. Who else can you ask for guidance from when you need the best advice possible?

3. How could you develop more supportive relationships in your life?

4. Describe a situation when you needed advice or guidance. How did consulting with this person help solve your problem?

IDENTIFYING SOURCES OF SUPPORT CIRCLE

CIRCLE ACTIVITY: *This activity will help you practice the concepts from today's learning circle.*

Directions:
- In the inner circle, list the people who support you 100%.
- In the second circle, list family and friends who would support you if you asked them.
- In the third circle, list people who would support you because it's part of their job.
- Outside of the circle, list any other people who would support you if you asked.

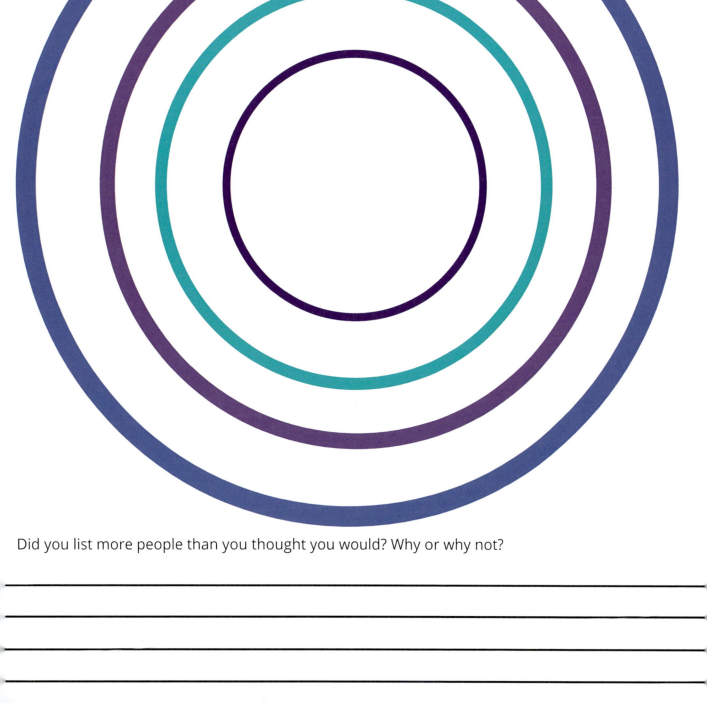

Did you list more people than you thought you would? Why or why not?

_____
_____
_____
_____

IDENTIFYING SOURCES OF SUPPORT CIRCLE

POST-CIRCLE: *Reflect on today's learning circle.*

1. Who else do you know who can give you the support and guidance you might need? Who came to your mind after listening to your peers as a source of support?

2. When your peers shared in learning circle, did you find you had anything in common with the type of person they rely upon for support and guidance?

3. How has getting the support, advice, and guidance of someone you trust made a difference in your life? What does that mean to you?

4. Describe a situation in which getting the support, advice, and guidance of someone you trust made the difference in your life.

MY NOTES

MY NOTES

MY NOTES

MY NOTES

MY NOTES

MY NOTES